OUR SENSES

How Taste Works

Sally Morgan

PowerKiDS
press™
New York

Published in 2011 by The Rosen Publishing Group Inc.
29 East 21st Street, New York, NY 10010

First Edition

Editor: Nicola Edwards
Designer: Robert Walster
Picture researcher: Shelley Noronha
Series consultant: Kate Ruttle
Design concept: Paul Cherrill

Library of Congress Cataloging-in-Publication Data

Morgan, Sally.
  How taste works / Sally Morgan. — 1st ed.
     p. cm. — (Our senses)
  Includes index.
  ISBN 978-1-61532-555-9 (library binding)
  ISBN 978-1-61532-563-4 (paperback)
  ISBN 978-1-61532-564-1 (6-pack)
  1. Taste—Juvenile literature. I. Title.
  QP456.M67 2011
  612.8'7—dc22

                           2009044496

Photographs:
Cover Dale Hogan/istock; title page Nina Matthews/istock; p4
Bananastock/Jupiter Media/ImagePick; p5 Comstock/ Jupiter
Media/ImagePick; p6 Dale Hogan/istock; p7 ©
M. Thomsen/zefa/Corbis; p8 Kasia Biel/istock; p9 Nina
Shannon/istock; p10 Andy Lim/Shutterstock; p11 Fritz
Polking/Ecoscene; p12 © Gareth Brown/Corbis; p13 ©
Norbert Schaefer/CORBIS; p14 Shutterstock; p15
Martyn f. Chillmaid; p16 Nina Matthews/istock;
p17 Ramona Heim/istock; p18 © Image Source/Corbis;
p19 Anna Ziska/istock; p20 © Robert Harding World;
p21 Rich Legg/istock; p22 Martyn f. Chillmaid; p23 (c)
Dorling Kindersley

Manufactured in China
CPSIA Compliance Information: Batch #WAS0102PK: For Further Information
contact Rosen Publishing, New York, New York at 1-800-237-9932

Web Sites

Due to the changing nature of Internet
links, PowerKids Press has developed
an online list of Web sites related to
the subject of this book. This site is
updated regularly. Please use this link
to access this list:
http://www.powerkidslinks.com/os/taste

Contents

Taste

We enjoy the food we eat because it is tasty. Imagine having to eat food every day that tasted of nothing.

Yum! Party foods taste good!

Taste is one of our five senses.
We taste food with our tongue.
When we chew food, the tongue
touches and tastes the food.

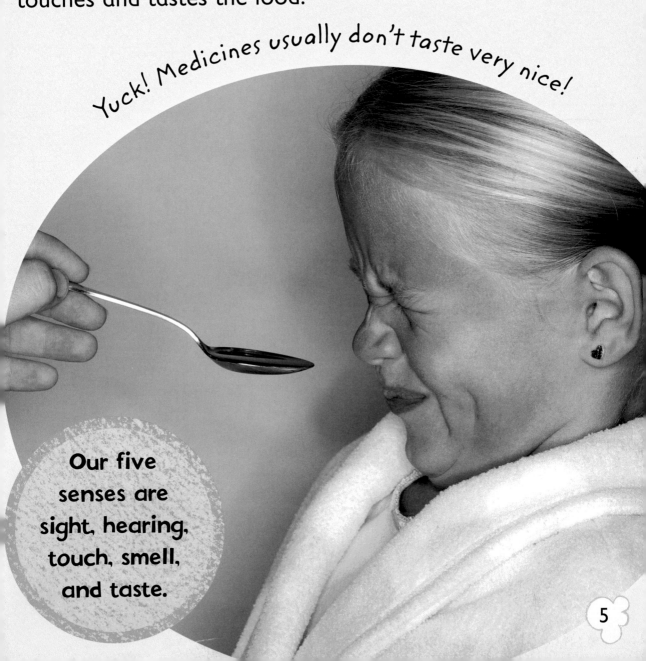

Yuck! Medicines usually don't taste very nice!

Our five
senses are
sight, hearing,
touch, smell,
and taste.

Taste Buds on the Tongue

Look in a mirror at your tongue. It is covered with lots of bumps. These bumps help you to grip your food.

You use your tongue to move food around your mouth and to lick your lips.

The bumps are covered in taste buds. Taste buds detect five different flavors—sweet, sour, bitter, salty, and something called umami (say oo-mah-mee), a savory taste.

There are about 10,000 taste buds on your tongue.

How Do Taste Buds Work?

Each taste bud is covered in very tiny hairs. When the hairs detect a flavor, they send a message to the brain.

Chilies give food a hot taste.

The hot taste of chili is really a feeling of pain on the tongue.

8

It is difficult to taste if you have a dry mouth. When you chew food, you produce saliva. Saliva helps you to taste and swallow your food.

A cold drink stops the taste buds from working so you cannot taste food so well.

Animals and Taste

Many animals have more taste buds than people. This gives them a much better sense of taste.

A catfish has taste buds all over its body.

Catfish have 10 times more taste buds than people.

Some animals, such as bears, taste with their tongue, as we do. Others taste with other parts of their bodies, such as their feet or tentacles.

The butterfly has hairs on its feet to taste leaves.

Sweet and Sour

Do you like the taste of cookies, cakes, and soft drinks? They contain sugar, which makes them taste sweet.

Cakes are made with sugar and may have a sugary topping, too.

Sour foods are sharp, acid-tasting foods. Lemon juice, rhubarb, and vinegar have a sour taste.

A grapefruit is a sour-tasting fruit.

Bitter and Salty

Some tastes, such as coffee and dark chocolate, are bitter. Many children do not like foods with a bitter taste.

Umami is a savory taste that is found in Chinese and Japanese foods.

Fish and other seafoods have a naturally salty taste. Some foods, for example, potato chips and bacon, have salt added to them.

Some people sprinkle salt on food to make it more tasty.

Too much salt is bad for your health.

15

Smell and Taste

When you put food in your mouth, its smell enters your nose from the back of your mouth. The smell of the food helps to you to identify its taste.

Your senses of smell and taste work together when you eat.

When your sense of smell isn't working well, such as when you have a cold, it makes it harder for you to taste things.

When you have a cold, you may sneeze a lot and your nose can become blocked.

Protecting your Body

Your sense of taste can protect you. Often, a food that is not safe to eat has a bad taste. When you put it in your mouth, its horrible taste makes you spit it out.

Milk that has spoiled has a nasty smell and a sour taste.

When the weather's hot, or when we exercise, our bodies sweat. Sweat contains water and salt. We have to eat and drink to replace them.

Exercising makes us thirsty.

Supertasters

Supertasters are people who have many more taste buds than other people. They can taste the tiniest flavors in food.

Supertasters can detect many different flavors in various types of tea.

Supertasters often do not enjoy bitter foods, such as coffee or spinach, because they are very sensitive to this taste.

A good sense of taste is very important for people who work as chefs.

More women are supertasters than men.

Your Sense of Taste

Try this taste test and see which breads you like.

You will need:
• different breads, such white, whole-wheat, p
Italian, nan, rye, sod
brioche, and bagel.
• a glass of water

Drink a sip of water and then take a small piece of bread. Feel the texture and then smell it. Now eat it. What flavors can you taste? Do this for each of the different breads, taking a sip of water first to remove the taste of other breads.

Which bread had the strongest flavor? Which bread did you like the most? Which bread did you like the least?

Confusing the Taste Buds

You will need:

• some slices of different foods, such as apple, orange, cheese, onion, and potato

Smell and taste are closely linked and it is easy to confuse your taste buds.

First, close your eyes, hold your nose, and try tasting a slice of each of the different foods. Don't swallow the foods you've tasted—spit them out into a paper towel. Try to figure out what each of the foods is. Can you taste the difference between a slice of apple and a slice of potato?

Now, hold a slice of orange under your nose and eat a piece of apple. What does the apple taste like? Try with this the other foods.

Glossary and Further Information

acid a sharp, sour taste. Vinegar and lemon juice have an acid taste

brain the control center of the body, found inside the head

saliva liquid produced in the mouth when you chew food

senses functions of the body through which we gather information about our surroundings

sensitive able to feel or detect something

supertaster someone who has more taste buds than usual, and a very good sense of taste

taste bud tiny bumps with hairs on the surface of the tongue that detect flavors

umami a savory taste found in Chinese and Japanese foods

Books

Animals And Their Senses: Animal Taste
by Kirsten Hall
(Weekly Reader Early Learning Library, 2005)
World of Wonder: Taste
Judy Wearing
(Weigl Publishers, 2009)
You Can't Taste Pickle With Your Ear
by Harriet Ziefert
(Blue Apple Books, 2006)

Index